EVERYTHING I NEED TO KNOW I LEARNED FROM WATCHING

The Office

AN UNOFFICIAL GUIDE

LIFE LESSONS AND
MANAGEMENT TIPS
INSPIRED BY
DUNDER MIFFLIN
PAPER COMPANY

TREVOR COURNEEN

The cast of *The Office* in a promotional photo for Season 3.

A Good Life Takes Work

From a short-lived but well-loved BBC series to one of the most iconic American sitcoms of all time to a worldwide phenomenon that continues to shape the zeitgeist, *The Office*, in its many forms, is here to stay. Whether being binged for the first time by newcomers or revisited for the umpteenth time by diehard fans, viewers gravitate toward this series about a fictional paper company because they know it's so much more than that. *The Office* shows us that "work-life balance," a concept that sounds good on (Dunder Mifflin) paper, is not always so cut and dried. For someone like Dwight, who's either toiling away on his beet farm or chasing a greater role at the company, work is life. For Jim and Pam, whose relationship experiences challenges ranging from periods of long distance to encroaching boom mic operators, life is work. With these examples and so many more, the series isn't just a source for cringetastic laughs, it's a guide for what to do—and maybe even more so, what not to do—when it comes to work, relationships and self-reflection. And while this book may not be Michael's unrealized business tome *Somehow I Manage*, it will hopefully still provide some meaningful insight inspired by the characters we love.

John Krasinski, B.J. Novak, Jenna Fischer, Steve Carell and Rainn Wilson in a promotional photo for *The Office* Season 1.

Rainn Wilson as Dwight and Steve Carell as Michael in "Dunder Mifflin Infinity" (S4E3).

A Little Improv Goes a Long Way

Wielded by both the characters and the actors who played them, improvisation is a skill that can serve you well in the workplace and beyond.

Whether you're a paper salesman, the owner of a refrigeration company or just an average Jim trying to get through everyday life, you're bound to encounter situations that call for quick thinking and adaptability. Improvisation is something everyone is capable of, regardless of our comedic pursuits. While Michael (Steve Carell) may think it merely represents an opportunity to pretend you're a trigger-happy detective, improv can also be a chance to seize a moment and change your fate.

In "Traveling Salesman" (S3E13), Michael and Andy (Ed Helms) meet with a client who has a photo of an impressive fish he caught on his desk. While Michael says he "never caught anything that big," Andy tries to impress the man by making up a story about the time he sniped an 80-pound shark off the coast of Montauk. It's a uniquely meta moment—both Andy and actor Ed Helms are improvising with the same goal of giving the Nard Dog a bigger bite. And in the Season 2 standout "Office Olympics" (S2E30), Rainn Wilson seized an opportunity to build the lore of Dwight's beet farm. According to the *Office Ladies* podcast, Dwight's brag that he "lives in a nine-bedroom farmhouse" was completely improvised, laying the groundwork for even more gags and character development. There's a lot to be gained by going off-script. Don't just say "yes" to the opportunities life provides—say "yes, and..."

Phyllis Smith as Phyllis and Rainn Wilson as Dwight in "Customer Survey" (S5E7).

Steve Carell as Michael in "The Dundies" (S2E1).

It Takes Time to Find Your Stride

"Sometimes I'll start a sentence and I don't even know where it's going. I just hope I find it along the way."

—MICHAEL

I n "The Duel" (S5E11), when David Wallace (Andy Buckley) asks him what the secret to his success is, Michael word vomits a delightfully odd response. But when he confesses the above quote to the camera afterward, he unknowingly reveals the philosophy that's been serving him so well: Just keep going until you figure things out.

The Office needed time to find its stride. When the series debuted, somewhat in the shadow of its British predecessor, eventual favorites like Kelly (Mindy Kaling), Meredith (Kate Flannery) and Creed (Creed Bratton) served as straight man-types to the main characters. Michael is little more than an offensive fool in Season 1, not yet showing many redeeming qualities. But soon enough, Michael helped the show find its way into the hearts of millions. Even if you find yourself fumbling through a new endeavor, keep fumbling. Eventually, you can feel like (or at least come across as) someone who knows what they're doing.

Rainn Wilson as Dwight in "The Meeting" (S6E2).

"Whenever I'm about to do something, I think, 'Would an idiot do that?' And if they would, I do not do that thing."

—Dwight,
"Business School" (S3E16)

We all make stupid mistakes sometimes—but what if there were an easy way to change that assumed fact of life? According to Dwight, the solution is simple. By just taking a beat (or a beet, in Dwight's case) to assess the situation and the choice you're about to make, you can oftentimes avoid doing something you'd be kicking yourself for later.

Communication Is Key

As *The Office*'s most iconic couple knows well, nothing can make or break a relationship quite like communication.

I t can be incredibly daunting to tell someone how you feel, whether those feelings are good or bad. The fear of how the other person will react is often the main obstacle to speaking from the heart, and if that fear isn't faced, it can drastically alter the fate of the relationship. Throughout the series, Jim and Pam demonstrate the beauty that can come from consistent communication as well as the pain that can result from its absence.

Early in the series, Jim (John Krasinski) is actually wise to withhold his true feelings for Pam (Jenna Fischer)—she's his coworker, they're good friends and she's engaged (albeit to an asshole). But rather than sweeping it all under the rug, Jim continues to strengthen their relationship through frequent communication, visiting the reception desk throughout the day, the week and the years to chat and make her laugh. When he finally confesses his love in "Casino Night" (S2E22), it's because he needed her to know out of fairness to himself, their friendship and the possibility of becoming something more.

Later in the series, though, Jim and Pam's marriage begins to suffer from a lack of communication. When Jim spends most of his time in Philadelphia to get his sports marketing company off the ground, he neglects to tell Pam some major information, including the amount of money he's invested. Pam, meanwhile, vents her frustrations and concerns to Brian the boom mic operator (Chris Diamantopoulos) rather than bringing them to Jim. When the two eventually agree to go home and have their overdue argument, it turns out to be the exact form of communication they needed. Whether it's a confession of love or an airing of grievances, know when it's time to speak your mind—it's often the only way to maintain a relationship.

John Krasinski as Jim and
Jenna Fischer as Pam in
"The Fire" (S2E4).

Rainn Wilson as
Dwight and Phyllis
Smith as Phyllis in
"Promos" (S9E18).

Don't Take Anything Too Seriously

Full of characters who aren't afraid to distract themselves from work, *The Office* illustrates the importance of lightening up.

What would *The Office* even be if every employee of Dunder Mifflin took a no-nonsense approach to their job? Would the fictional documentary crew continue to film such straitlaced individuals in this drab setting? Throughout the series, the characters demonstrate time and again that no matter where you are and what you're doing, you can always find ways to have fun.

Michael, of course, deserves much of the credit for making a paper company in Scranton, Pennsylvania, a fun (and often unpredictable) place to work. Despite being the manager, he's typically the one discouraging productivity. Jim, despite having the potential for a promotion, typically opts to amuse himself by pranking Dwight rather than focusing on making sales. There's a designated party planning committee, an Office Olympics and even an annual awards ceremony to honor anything but work-related achievements. The employees of Dunder Mifflin Scranton recognize that since the workplace and the people in it take up at least 40 hours of their time week after week, they might as well make the most of it and fit in some fun.

There are plenty of things in life you should take seriously, but whether you notice or not, there are also plenty of opportunities to loosen up a little. Sometimes, that's all you can do to maintain sanity as you go through the same routines over and over again.

Ed Helms as Andy and Rainn Wilson as Dwight in "Local Ad" (S4E5).

Brian Baumgartner as Kevin in "The Return" (S3E14).

"Why waste time
say lot word when
few word do trick?"

—Kevin,
"The Incentive" (S8E2)

This frequently quoted line from Dunder Mifflin's guileless accountant
(Brian Baumgartner) proves being economical doesn't just apply to money. While
he may not have the hang of this approach, Kevin does have the right idea.
Everyone's time is precious. If you've got something to say, get to the point.

Steve Carell
as Michael in
Season 4 of
The Office.

Use Confidence Responsibly

"Confidence: It's the food of the wise man but the liquor of the fool."
—VIKRAM, "DREAM TEAM" (S5E22)

When the series introduces us to Vikram (Ranjit Chowdhry), he's working as a telemarketer—a job that requires a lot of confidence. Later, when Michael recruits him for the fledgling Michael Scott Paper Company, Vikram offers this nugget, proving he understands that Spider-Man's uncle was right about power and responsibility.

The Office is full of moments of self-assuredness causing self-destruction, but few episodes demonstrate this like the two-part Season 3 finale "The Job" (S3E24 and S3E25). Certain he's going to get the corporate gig he, Jim and Karen (Rashida Jones) are all applying for, Michael sells his condo and names Dwight his successor as regional manager. And when hiring for the role, David Wallace goes too bold: Even though Ryan (B.J. Novak) has never made a sale, David hires him because he has a business administration degree (for a reminder of how this pans out, see pg. 98). Listen to Vikram—it's possible to have too much of a good thing, and confidence is definitely one of those things.

Paul Lieberstein as Toby in
"The Negotiation" (S3E19).

You Can't Win Everyone's Friendship

The Office reminds us that no matter how charming or kind you are, some people just can't be won over.

The employees of Dunder Mifflin Scranton are a tight-knit group. Working in such close quarters is bound to bring people together on a personal level—but that proximity also makes it easier for people to get on each other's nerves.

Michael and Toby's relationship is a bottomless well of comedy and an example of just how unbalanced a workplace relationship can be. Despite the fact that Toby (Paul Lieberstein) is merely doing his job (often half-heartedly) as an HR representative, Michael can only see him as an enemy, the fun police there to prevent him from being himself. Exhibit A: Toby's refusal to let Michael present a giant check to a group of Boy Scouts in "Casino Night" (S2E22) because "there's gambling and alcohol and it's in our dangerous warehouse." Even though the pair appear to reach tiny breakthroughs at points in the series, things always come crashing down. As Michael succinctly puts it in "Casino Night," "Honestly, every time I try to do something fun or exciting, you make it not that way."

Even Jim—designed to be the likable everyman viewers can relate to and root for—isn't immune to being arbitrarily disliked by a coworker. While his tuxedo and confusion about a "rundown" don't help, Jim's affability has no effect on new branch manager Charles Miner (Idris Elba) in Season 5, whose dead-serious approach clashes with Jim's more casual attitude. It goes to show that even if you believe you're doing everything right, someone can always come along and find plenty of wrong. Try to take it with a grain of salt.

Steve Carell as Michael and Paul Lieberstein as Toby in "The Deposition" (S4E12).

Steve Carell as Michael and Leslie David Baker as Stanley in "Initiation" (S3E5).

Have Something to Look Forward To

"I wake up every morning in a bed that's too small, drive my daughter to a school that's too expensive and then I go to work to a job for which I get paid too little. But on Pretzel Day, well, I like Pretzel Day."
—STANLEY, "INITIATION" (S3E5)

n "Initiation" (S3E5), Stanley (Leslie David Baker) smiles more than he does in nearly any other episode. The reason? It's Pretzel Day. Though he seemingly doesn't have many sources of happiness in his life, a free soft pretzel is something Stanley can look forward to every year. In fact, he enjoys it so much he's even happy to eat with Michael and drop a "That's what she said."

Stanley isn't the only one who relies on a certain day of the year to bring unbridled joy. In "St. Patrick's Day" (S6E19), Meredith interrupts an argument between Kelly and Ryan for the sake of her favorite holiday. "Stop fighting!" she insists. "Just on St. Patrick's Day, OK? Just one perfect day a year. No hassles. No problems. No kids." Hold tight to life's simple pleasures. They may seem small to others, but anything guaranteed to make you happy is a big deal.

Steve Carell as Michael in "Dunder Mifflin Infinity" (S4E2).

"You miss 100 percent of the shots you don't take."

—Wayne Gretzky
—Michael Scott, "Michael Scott Paper Company" (S5E23)

While shamelessly skating on an aphorism famously uttered by one of the greatest players in any sport, Michael does have good reason to apply this quote to himself in "Michael Scott Paper Company" (S5E23). The goofball manager never lets risks such as embarrassment or failure stop him from just going for it, whether it's a joke that might not land or, in this case, a bold business idea that could easily blow up in his face. When it comes to taking chances, be like Michael. And Wayne.

Ed Helms as Andy in "Promos" (S9E18).

Face Your Problems Head On...

"What we have here is the ultimate smackdown between the Nard Dog and crippling despair, loneliness and depression. I intend to win."

—ANDY, "LECTURE CIRCUIT" (S5E16)

A ndy is no stranger to emotions getting the best of him (the hole in the wall says hi, Nard Dog), which might be why he's so determined to overcome his struggles in "Lecture Circuit: Part 1" (S5E16). When he makes the declaration above, Andy is fresh off the heels of facing a major problem: Angela's (Angela Kinsey) affair with Dwight.

In "The Duel" (S5E11), after being the last to learn his fiancée is cheating, Andy confronts Angela and Dwight, which leads to the two salesmen having an embarrassing showdown in the parking lot. Though Andy is technically confronting this problem from behind the wheel of his Prius, he's still facing it. So when he says he plans to defeat his demons a few episodes later, he's able to make that statement with conviction. It's never easy to get back on track after enduring unfortunate events, but it's always worth the effort.

John Krasinski as Jim in "The Meeting" (S6E2).

...But the Occasional Distraction Can Be Helpful

"I think today was a good day to have two managers. 'Cause if you're a family stuck on a lifeboat in the middle of the ocean, one parent might want to just keep rowing. But if the other parent wants to play a game, it's not because they're crazy. It's because they're doing it for the kids."

—JIM, "MURDER" (S6E10)

After word gets out that Dunder Mifflin is in serious financial trouble in "Murder" (S6E10), anxiety looms as everyone wonders if their jobs are in jeopardy. Never one to let bad morale linger, Michael makes everyone play the murder mystery game *Belles, Bourbon and Bullets* to keep their minds off the news.

The game gradually becomes a hit among the employees, save for newly appointed comanager Jim, who fears they're ignoring important work at a crucial time. Eventually, Michael snaps at Jim's attempts to return to reality, telling him the employees need the game to get them through this difficult day, and Jim learns a lesson anyone can benefit from: When you can't control a bad outcome, sometimes it's best to just try and take your mind off it for a while.

Kate Flannery as Meredith, B.J. Novak as Ryan and Jenna Fischer as Pam in *The Office* Season 6.

Oscar Nuñez as Oscar, Zach Woods as Gabe and Kate Flannery as Meredith in "Christmas Wishes" (S8E10).

> "You gotta be able to laugh at yourself. I'm one of the gang."
>
> —Gabe,
> "Secretary's Day" (S6E20)

As he tries to assert his authority without immediately making himself everyone's enemy in "Secretary's Day" (S6E20), Gabe (Zach Woods) inevitably becomes the butt of the joke. Mocked for his gangly appearance and his bizarre use of the word "ciao," Sabre's coordinating director for emerging regions states the importance of laughing at yourself—which is true, whether he believes it or not. Taking a joke at your own expense can thicken your skin for tougher blows in the future.

Rainn Wilson as Dwight in "The Fight" (S2E6).

Your Job Doesn't Define You

The Office provides frequent reminders that people lead interesting lives independent of what they do from 9 to 5.

With all that happens beyond the walls of the titular office, it's sometimes easy to forget that the very premise of the series is a documentary about people working at a paper company. Perhaps that's exactly why the crew continued filming for so many years—the unique individuals employed at Dunder Mifflin Scranton constantly prove that people are much more than their job titles.

When we first see these characters in the earliest episodes, there's little to suggest who they are when they're off the clock. But as the series progresses, viewers are given a much more vivid picture of these personalities. Michael craves a brighter spotlight, spending his free time learning magic tricks and taking improv classes. Pam dreams of pursuing a more rewarding, creative career, displaying her paintings at an exhibit and taking any opportunity to incorporate her artistic abilities into her day job. Andy, Kevin and Darryl (Craig Robinson) are all musically gifted, combining their talents to form a band in the warehouse. And Dwight, of course, is not only a martial arts enthusiast but also a successful beet farmer/bed and breakfast owner who could just as easily be making his living that way.

Next time someone making small talk asks, "What do you do?" consider telling them about your hobbies or passions rather than your occupation. It's always easier to talk about the things you love.

Craig Robinson as Darryl and Ed Helms as Andy in "The Sting" (S7E5).

Steve Carell as
Michael Scott (as
Michael Scarn)
in "Threat Level
Midnight" (S7E17).

Embrace Your Flaws

"Guess what? I have flaws. What are they? Oh, I don't know,
I sing in the shower, sometimes I spend too much time volunteering.
Occasionally I'll hit somebody with my car. So sue me."

—MICHAEL, "FUN RUN" (S4E1)

After hitting Meredith with his car in "Fun Run" (S4E1), Michael tries to blame the incident on a "curse." Later, when he's exhausted on the ground during the 5K held in Meredith's honor (more on pg. 122), he embraces the fact that he's not, in fact, "very fast" like Forrest Gump and his mistake was indeed the cause of all this. With that admission, he's able to hobble to the finish line.

Later in the series, Michael faces his flaws again when he screens his movie in "Threat Level Midnight" (S7E17). When some employees (despite starring in the amateur action film themselves) start snickering at the unintentional comedy of *Threat Level Midnight*, Michael storms off. But after talking to Holly (Amy Ryan), he returns to the screening with a new attitude and even begins laughing at the plot and continuity errors himself. Once you acknowledge your flaws, you're able to present a more complete picture of yourself—a person who knows there are still areas in which they can improve.

Jenna Fischer as Pam in "Drug Testing" (S2E20).

"There's a lot of beauty in ordinary things."

—Pam,
"Finale Part 1 and Part 2"
(S9E26)

In the final moments of *The Office*, Pam perfectly sums up the series. Remarking how she gradually understood why the documentary crew chose to follow a paper company, she delivers her true artist statement over a flashback of Michael hanging her painting of the office building. It's a reminder that the parts of life that seem mundane can eventually become the most meaningful.

Be Prepared So You Don't Panic

Under the impression that they're facing an actual emergency, the employees of Dunder Mifflin remind us that poor preparation can result in utter chaos.

"**S**tress Relief Part 1" (S5E14) features perhaps the most iconic cold open of the series, in which Dwight tries to teach his coworkers the importance of fire safety by starting an actual fire in the office. "People learn in lots of different ways," the eccentric salesman says ominously. "But experience is the best teacher." The events that follow are basically Murphy's Law in action.

As Dwight asks everyone what the procedure is, a cloud of fearful confusion thicker than the billowing smoke fills the room, leading to Michael screaming at everyone to stay calm (spoiler: They don't). Oscar (Oscar Nuñez) tries to escape through the ceiling; Kevin smashes the vending machine and grabs everything he can; Andy cries out that the fire is "shooting" at them and Michael, believing he's trapped, throws a projector through his office window. By the time Dwight announces it was all a test, the panic has already reached irreversible levels as Stanley begins to have a heart attack.

While Dwight's approach is objectively terrible, he was able to prove his suspicion that the employees of Dunder Mifflin Scranton were completely ill-prepared for an emergency. As Michael puts it, "I knew exactly what to do. But in a much more real sense, I had no idea what to do." Though it's difficult to know precisely how you'd fare in a scary situation, your best bet is to be as prepared as possible so you don't panic to the point of harming yourself or those around you.

Rainn Wilson as Dwight, Jenna Fischer as Pam, Steve Carell as Michael, John Krasinski as Jim and B.J. Novak as Ryan in a promotional photo for Season 5

Melora Hardin as Jan in "The Negotiation" (S3E19).

"There are always a million reasons not to do something."

—Jan,
"Boys and Girls" (S2E15)

When offering this advice to a conflicted Pam in "Boys and Girls" (S2E15), Jan (Melora Hardin), of all people, is actually quite wise. This is a much more calm and collected Jan, still a few years away from disregarding the reasons not to throw a Dundie at a tiny TV. But here, she's right—you shouldn't bother looking for excuses to avoid chasing your dreams, because you will find them. Instead, just go for it. Even if it's candle making.

Steve Carell as Michael in "The Dundies" (S2E1).

Small Victories Deserve Celebration

The characters of *The Office* hold tight to the belief that even if it may not seem so significant to others, a win's a win.

I t can be hard to feel like you're "winning" when you're going through the same routines week after week. But if you start to look a little closer every day, you may notice the little things you're doing right. And as the employees of Dunder Mifflin know, those small victories are not insignificant.

In "Goodbye, Toby" (S4E14), when a construction crew starts taking up several parking spaces, the likes of Kevin and Andy are forced to park in a distant lot. When Michael won't help them fix the issue, they boldly call a meeting with the bosses of Scranton Business Park. "We want our parking spaces back!" Kevin declares before pitifully telling the men that the long walk from the satellite lot causes "some people" to "sweat too much for comfort." The strategy works, resulting in a heartwarming smile on Kevin's face as he tells the documentary crew, "It's nice to win one."

Though they may not have quite as much enthusiasm as Michael, the employees of Dunder Mifflin Scranton do enjoy celebrating the occasion that is their boss's annual awards ceremony. In "The Dundies" (S2E1), Stanley sets his usual prickliness aside to accept his "Fine Work" award, chuckling, "At least I didn't get 'Smelliest Bowel Movement' like Kevin." Pam, though a tad intoxicated, makes a big deal out of winning the "Whitest Sneakers Award," giving an impassioned speech and even stealing a smooch from Jim. As Oscar puts it, "The Dundies are kind of like a kid's birthday party. You go and there's really nothing for you to do there, but the kid's having a really good time." The fact that Michael is able to host such an event, honor his employees and do his comedy bits in a Chili's is a victory in itself. Take the occasional victory lap, even if the win isn't obvious to others.

Brian Baumgartner as Kevin in "Stairmageddon" (S9E20).

From left: Angela Kinsey as Angela, Brian Baumgartner as Kevin, Will Ferrell as Deangelo Vickers, Jenna Fischer as Pam, Steve Carell as Michael and John Krasinski as Jim in "Training Day" (S7E20).

SUITE 100
Ruben's Electrical
Electrical Con...

Steve Carell as Michael and
Leslie David Baker as Stanley
in "Initiation" (S3E5).

Don't Spill the Beans

"How do you untell something? You can't.
You can't put words back in your mouth."

—MICHAEL, "GOSSIP" (S6E1)

As Michael explains in "Gossip" (S6E1), you can't put the lid back on spilled beans (for a more literal version of this, see pg. 118). After learning of Stanley's possible affair from the interns, Michael immediately goes around telling everyone in the office. By the time he talks to Stanley—who confirms he's been seeing his nurse, Cynthia (Algerita Wynn), on the side—it's too late to keep the information secret, as the mustachioed salesman requests. Michael then tries to do damage control by spreading false rumors, but his attempts are ruined while on the phone with Stanley's wife, Teri (Joanne Carlsen), whom he mistakenly calls "Cynthia." He then sees how loose lips sink not only ships but also land vessels as Stanley destroys his boss's car with a tire iron.

Modern forms of communication allow us to edit, unsend and delete much of what we say, but verbal exchanges remain permanent. Before you speak a thought into existence, be sure you shouldn't bite your tongue instead.

John Krasinski as Jim and Ed Helms as Andy in "Product Recall" (S3E21).

"I'm always thinking one step ahead, like a carpenter who makes stairs."

—Andy,
"The Merger" (S3E8)

Viewers were still getting to know Ivy League songster Andy Bernard when "The Merger" (S3E8) first aired, but this classic quote from that episode certainly sped up the process. Andy shows us that when you put solid forethought into things—clothing choices, nicknames, grand romantic gestures—you're able to move through the world with confidence. If you're not spending a little time considering your next step, you run a greater risk of tripping yourself up.

Phyllis Smith as Phyllis in "Ben Franklin" (S3E15).

You Never Know Where a Career Path Will Take You

Through events on-screen and off-, *The Office* proves a job can change your life in many different ways.

S ometimes, a job is just a job. It helps you put food on the table, pay the bills and ensure others know you were in an a cappella group at Cornell. But once in a while, a job can be the catalyst that forever changes your life.

When Phyllis Smith showed up to work at the pilot screen test for *The Office*, she wasn't there to play the saleswoman who would one day marry Bob Vance (Bob Vance, Vance Refrigeration). Instead, she was working as a casting agent. But when Smith began reading lines, the show's executive producers were so impressed they essentially created the Phyllis character on the spot. In a similar instance of a day job leading to NBC sitcom fame overnight, Andy Buckley—known to fans for his role as Dunder Mifflin's CFO, David Wallace—was working as a stockbroker for Merrill Lynch when he ran into casting director Allison Jones at a grocery store. Buckley had a brief run as an actor but believed those days were behind him when he took the corporate gig. As it turned out, though, his real-life experience in the field made him a perfect fit to play one of Michael Scott's C-suite antagonists.

Many characters on *The Office* have also been able to enjoy big life changes thanks to their chosen career paths. Jim and Pam, Michael and Holly and Dwight and Angela all meet working at Dunder Mifflin and end up married. Ryan, despite starting as a temp, ascends straight to the company's corporate offices in NYC (see pg. 98). Whether it helps you skip a few steps en route to your dream job or leads you to the love of your life, a professional pursuit can take you to some unexpected places. Don't be afraid to take the journey.

Andy Buckley as David Wallace in "Couples Discount" (S9E15).

Ed Helms as Andy and
Ellie Kemper as Erin in
"Fundraiser" (S8E22).

"I'm not going to be one of those exes who can't move on. They have their life and I have mine..."

—Erin,
"Pool Party" (S8E12)

Erin (Ellie Kemper) isn't typically someone the other employees turn to for wisdom, but the lovable receptionist does seem to know how to handle a breakup with surprising maturity in "Pool Party" (S8E12). When relationships fall apart, it's natural to want to pick up the pieces and force them back together with glue, tape, staples or anything else you can get from the office supply closet. Instead, take the opportunity to focus on finding exciting new ways to spend your time. You're whole as you are.

Creed Bratton a Creed in "Benihan Christmas" (S3E10)

Nonchalance Can Be Liberating

"I stopped caring a long time ago."

— CREED, "CASINO NIGHT" (S2E22)

Though we see him do very little work throughout the series, it's quite fitting that Creed is in charge of quality assurance. Creed is the epitome of a free spirit, a man who clearly marches to the beat of a very jazzy drummer only he can hear. Thanks to his many years of experience on Earth, the former hippie and (real-life) musician knows that when you stop caring about issues that are ultimately irrelevant to your well-being, the quality of your life becomes much more assured.

Of course, not everyone can be exactly like Creed (nor should they). Even the most laid-back among us know there are still plenty of things in life that are worth worrying about. Your best bet is to try not to sweat the small stuff—before you know it, you'll be an offbeat senior citizen who's blissfully unbothered by the things that don't matter in the long run.

John Krasinski as Jim, Jenna Fischer as Pam, Rainn Wilson as Dwight, Brian Baumgartner as Kevin and Creed Bratton as Creed in "Dwight Christmas" (S9E9).

Ed Helms as Andy and James Spader as Robert California in "Doomsday" (S8E6).

"I'll tell you some things I find unproductive: Constantly worrying about where you stand based on inscrutable social cues, and then inevitably reframing it all in a reassuring way so that you can get to sleep at night."

—Robert California, "The List" (S8E1)

The enigmatic, self-proclaimed "Lizard King" of *The Office* (James Spader) may have had a short tenure as well as some uniquely strange takes, but he does offer up sage advice in "The List" (S8E1). It may be impossible to truly not care what others think of you, but you can do yourself a favor by trying not to dwell on every supposed social faux pas. Chances are you're the only one still thinking about those moments, so cut yourself some slack.

Dunder Mifflin Scranton employees hold a funeral for a bird in "Grief Counseling" (S3E4).

Give Yourself Space to Grieve

"Society teaches us that having feelings and crying is bad and wrong. Well, that's baloney, because grief isn't wrong. There's such a thing as good grief. Just ask Charlie Brown."

—MICHAEL, "GRIEF COUNSELING" (S3E4)

After hearing his former boss Ed Truck (Ken Howard) has died by decapitation in "Grief Counseling" (S3E4), Michael insists his employees dive headfirst (sorry, Ed) into grief counseling exercises. While the session doesn't go as planned—Pam, Ryan and Kevin recite movie plots instead of personal stories of loss—Michael gets another chance to unite the crew in mourning. Devastated by the discovery of a dead bird in the parking lot, he holds a funeral for the fallen creature, during which Pam reads a poem and Dwight plays his recorder. Most importantly, Michael lets the tears flow. Despite trying to force feelings out of his employees all day, he was the one who needed to grieve. When faced with loss, give yourself permission to feel. It's the only way to find catharsis.

Ricky Gervais as David Brent in the BBC's *The Office*.

There's Always Room for Humor

"When people say to me, 'Would you rather be thought of as a funny man or a great boss?' My answer's always the same: To me, they're not mutually exclusive."

—DAVID BRENT, "MERGER" (S2E1)

Before Michael Scott was disregarding professionalism in favor of comedy bits, David Brent was doing the very same on the BBC's *The Office.* Played by Ricky Gervais, cocreator and cowriter of the U.K. series, David's above statement reveals exactly why this character could so easily be adapted for audiences in America (or Germany, India or any of the other 12 countries with their own iterations of the series). To David, being a "great boss" means being quick with a quip to ensure your employees adore you (something he blindly believes). Across the pond in Scranton, Michael has a similar philosophy—and he's ultimately proven right. On his last day at Dunder Mifflin, after years of antics and groan-worthy bits, he gets to hear Jim tearfully dub him the "best boss I ever had." Even if you're not always amazing at what you do, the ability to make people laugh can set you apart from the aloof workaholics of the world.

B.J. Novak as Ryan in "The Return" (S3E14).

> "I don't need
> a judge to tell
> me to keep my
> community clean."
>
> —Ryan,
> "Weight Loss" (S5E1)

Though he's absolutely being facetious with this statement about his court-ordered community service in "Weight Loss" (S5E1), Ryan verbalizes a mentality that would be admirable if only it were sincere. At this point in the series, we've seen enough of the corrupt, former corporate hotshot to know he's not picking up trash because he actually believes in the betterment of his community. Don't be like Ryan and do a good deed because social expectations or authority figures call for it: Do the right thing because it's the right thing to do.

Ed Helms as Andy and Angela Kinsey as Angela in "Local Ad" (S4E9).

Consequences Will Catch Up to You

One of *The Office*'s most dysfunctional couples proves karma is often hot on the trail of those who do wrong.

The employees of Dunder Mifflin Scranton get away with countless acts of unprofessional behavior, but they rarely have to worry about their jobs being in danger as a result (otherwise Jim would have likely been fired during the series's pilot). When the characters make poor personal decisions, however, they do tend to pay the price eventually. For proof, look no further than the messy saga of Dwight and Angela.

When "Monkey" asks "D" to take care of her ailing cat Sprinkles in "Fun Run" (S4E1), the oddball beet farmer, unfortunately, does exactly that. Though Dwight claims he found the feline already deceased, Angela rightfully suspects he euthanized her. "Sprinkles's body was in the freezer, where Dwight said he left her," she tells Pam. "But all my bags of frozen french fries had been clawed to shreds!" Dwight's devastating decision gets him dumped, and Angela soon begins a relationship with Andy. But bad habits die hard, and the Nard Dog eventually learns his fiancée is cheating on him with her old flame (see pg. 34). A couple of years later, the shoe is on the other foot when Angela finds out what it's like to lose a partner to a coworker. "Robert seems great," Oscar says in "Classy Christmas" (S7E11), foreshadowing his future affair with Angela's state senator husband. "He's very handsome, firm handshake, he's gay, good sense of humor."

Despite all the pain they caused throughout their years together and apart, for better or worse, the only people Dwight and Angela could possibly end up with were each other. You may come out on top in the end, but hurtful actions can haunt you until the karmic debt is repaid. Only then will you find a happy ending.

Rainn Wilson as Dwight and Angela Kinsey as Angela in "Finale Part 1 and Part 2" (S9E26).

Angela Kinsey as Angela, Kate Flannery as Meredith, Oscar Nuñez as Oscar, Jenna Fischer as Pam and Ellie Kemper as Erin in "Sex Ed" (S7E4).

"Sometimes I get so bored I just want to scream, and then sometimes I actually do scream. I just sort of feel out what the situation calls for."

—Kelly,
"After Hours" (S8E16)

Kelly is rarely one to ignore her whims, no matter how inappropriate they may be. But in the privacy of your own home, your car or even a private office with the door closed tight, why not be like Kelly and give in to that primal urge to let frustration fly in the form of a guttural scream? It might seem a little unhinged, but you'll undoubtedly get the catharsis you're looking for.

Rainn Wilson as Dwight in "Garden Party" (S8E4).

Know Your Family Tree

**Like any good farmer, Dwight knows
it's never wise to disregard your roots.**

While plenty of personal details about each character are
revealed across nine seasons, no one on *The Office* is a
more complete picture than Dwight K. Schrute. Some of
the yellow-shirted salesman's backstory is owed to Rainn Wilson's
improv skills (see pg. 6), and to the writers for taking those seeds and
growing them into bountiful crops of evergreen comedy. And while
his many quirks are endlessly entertaining, Dwight's best trait is that
despite how bizarre he may seem to anyone whose last name isn't
Schrute, he is unwaveringly proud of who he is.

Whether the subject is weddings, funerals or holidays, Dwight is always eager to chime in with Schrute family traditions, from getting married standing in your own grave to shooting a corpse in a casket to ensure they're dead to determining if children have been "impish or admirable" at Christmastime. He never pauses to consider how antiquated or unappealing some of these traditions are, instead always offering them with complete conviction. And though most mentions of Dwight's childhood sound absurdly harsh (he was once shunned by his family for not saving excess tuna can oil), he seems to credit his strict upbringing with giving him the discipline to become a top salesman, a successful beet farmer/B&B owner and a (mediocre) martial artist.

Though Dwight may disagree, it's also important to know your family's history in case you can avoid repeating any of their mistakes (don't go the Schrute route and shun a relative over some minor error, for example). You can be proud of your roots while still allowing yourself to grow freely.

Rainn Wilson as Dwight and
John Krasinski as Jim in
"Garden Party" (S8E4).

Ricky Gervais as David and Mackenzie Crook as Gareth in *The Office* (BBC).

"I did learn a lot from David. I learnt from his mistakes."

—Gareth Keenan, "Christmas Special: Part I" (S3E1)

David Brent is not the type of manager everyone should aspire to be, but he still provides his employees with plenty of valuable lessons (most of them being examples of what not to do). If you find yourself looking to others for inspiration, be sure to observe not just the good, but also the bad and the ugly. All aspects are equally educational.

B.J. Novak as Ryan
in Season 3.

Power Corrupts Quickly

If you're moving up in the world, be sure to keep your ego in check—looking at you, Ryan.

Holding a high-ranking position at a paper company may not seem so prestigious in the grand scheme of corporate America, but *The Office* shows us that any taste of "power" has the potential to go straight to someone's head. The David Wallaces of Dunder Mifflin may wield their authority responsibly, but then there's Ryan Howard, who proves no match for the corrupting capabilities of corporate life in the Big Apple. From temp worker to VP of Sales, Ryan's sudden rise to the top is easily overshadowed by his swift, embarrassing downfall.

The moment Ryan finds out he got the corporate gig in the final moments of "The Job" (S3E23), he has a look in his eyes unlike any viewers had seen from him before. Up until this point, the only time the business school grad seemed dangerous was when he accidentally started a fire in the office's toaster oven. But after moving to New York City with an impressive new title attached to his name and a Bluetooth headset placed firmly in his ear, Ryan dives head first into the nightlife, desperately trying to reshape his image into that of a hotshot playboy. In hopes of illustrating the necessary maturity for the job, he grows a bristly beard (which Oscar dubs a "crime.") And then he commits an actual crime: Not long after stepping into the role, Ryan is convicted of fraud for misleading Dunder Mifflin's shareholders, which results in a humiliating public arrest his former coworkers at Scranton get to witness thanks to YouTube.

Even if you think you're immune to the pitfalls of supposed power, try to stay grateful so you can stay humble. Otherwise, you might end up doing court-ordered community service and hoping your old boss gets desperate enough to hire you back.

B.J. Novak as Ryan and Jenna Fischer as Pam in Season 6.

Ricky Gervais as David in
The Office (BBC) episode
"Charity" (S2E5).

Take a Break When You Need One

"I can wake up one morning and go, 'I don't feel like working today. Can I stay in bed?' 'You'd better ask the boss.' 'David, can I stay in bed?' 'Yes, David.' Both me. Not me in bed with another bloke called David."

—DAVID BRENT, "INTERVIEW" (S2E6)

Given his general approach to work, this quote from David Brent may sound like a classic example of a slacker mindset. And, well, that may be true. But whether or not he realizes it, the Wernham Hogg Slough general manager is actually tapping into something a bit deeper here: the importance of self-care.

It's not just David who subscribes to this philosophy; the U.S. version of *The Office* is full of instances of characters choosing R&R over responsibilities, from exhausted parents Pam and Jim finding a place to nap in the warehouse to Michael sleeping on his desk after inhaling a massive chicken pot pie. Regardless of your role at work, when it comes to your own well-being, you're the boss. Be sure to give yourself the occasional day off when you need it.

The employees of Dunder Mifflin Scranton practice tai chi in "Finale Part 1 and Part 2" (S9E26).

Rainn Wilson as Dwight and B.J. Novak as Ryan in "Gossip" (S6E1).

"Not everything's a lesson, Ryan, sometimes you just fail."

—Dwight, "Initiation" (S3E5)

When Ryan blows his first sales call in "Initiation" (S3E5), Dwight delivers this hard truth without pulling the punch. And though he's claiming there's no takeaway in this case, Dwight's statement is a valuable lesson in itself. Life won't always go your way, and not every mishap is guaranteed to provide valuable insight into preventing similar failures in the future.

David Denman as
Roy in Season 3.

People Can Change

**Even some of the most unlikeable characters on
The Office manage to gradually become better people.**

Running for nine robust seasons, *The Office* managed to pull off the rare TV feat of not wearing out its welcome. Today, fans who religiously watched the series as it originally aired are still eagerly binging season after season, reliving their favorite moments. While there are many factors contributing to this longevity, much of it is thanks to the show featuring an ensemble of characters that just keeps growing—both in size and collective maturity.

While there's never a true, lasting antagonist in the series, the early seasons certainly encourage viewers to root against Roy (David

Denman). It's painfully clear he doesn't fully appreciate Pam, and he definitely deserves the wrath of Dwight's pepper spray when he tries to attack Jim in "The Negotiation" (S3E19). But a couple of seasons later, when Roy runs into Jim at the bar in "Crime Aid" (S5E5), Roy extends his hand and congratulates his ex-fiancée's new fiancé (though some of his paranoid tendencies still seem to linger). And in "Roy's Wedding" (S9E2), the former warehouse worker truly shows off his transformation when he surprises his bride (and even more so, Jim and Pam) by performing Billy Joel's "She's Got a Way."

Further proving that final season nuptials have a way of bringing out the best in everyone, Dwight and Angela's wedding in "Finale Part 1 and Part 2" (S9E26) is filled with heartwarming moments of character growth. Dwight chooses Jim to be his best man, Angela quickly apologizes to Phyllis after snapping at her and then there's Michael, who, in stark contrast to his spotlight-stealing antics at Phyllis's wedding, is just happy to be Dwight's surprise best man (completing Jim's finest prank ever) and proudly watch the ceremony. While it certainly doesn't apply to everyone, people can change for the better—as long as they truly want to.

David Denman as Roy in "The Negotiation" (S3E19).

Creed Bratton as Creed, Rainn Wilson as Dwight and Craig Robinson as Darryl in "Jury Duty" (S8E13).

Take the Occasional Risk

"Nerf ball. You live a sweet little Nerfy life, sittin' on your biscuit, never having to risk it."

—DARRYL, "SAFETY TRAINING" (S3E20)

When Michael hears these words from Darryl in "Safety Training" (S3E20), he takes the word "risk" a bit too literally and soon devises a plan to stage a leap from the office rooftop. But while Darryl's right in that the non-warehouse employees of Dunder Mifflin Scranton don't have to deal with physical safety hazards on a regular basis, many of them do "risk it" from time to time.

In one swift leap of faith in "The Job, Part 2" (S3E25), Jim bails on a big job opportunity, breaks up with Karen and asks Pam out on a date—and it pays off! Later in the series, Pam takes a major risk of her own when she spontaneously follows Michael out of the office and into the unknown of the Michael Scott Paper Company. While the fate of that company is somewhat complicated (more on this on pg. 144), Pam undoubtedly feels validated as the move allows her to leave her receptionist days behind to prove herself as a saleswoman. Not every opportunity comes on a sweet little Nerfy platter. Sometimes you have to get off your biscuit and take risks to make things happen.

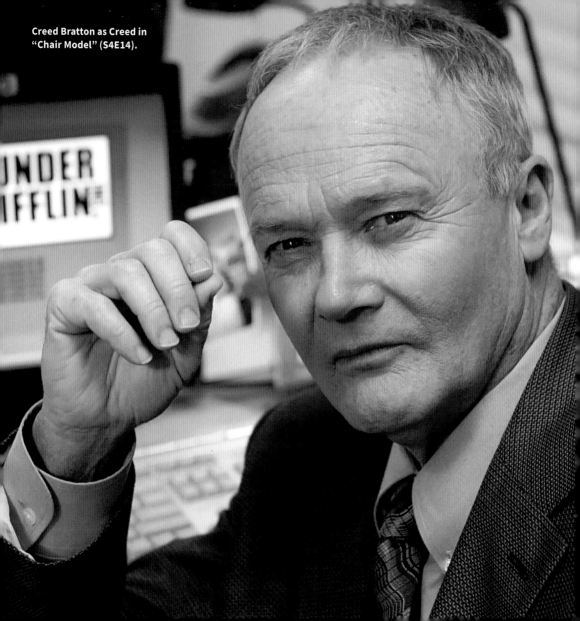

Set Achievable Goals

"I wanna do a cartwheel. But real casual-like. Not enough to make a big deal out of it, but I know everyone saw it. One stunning, gorgeous cartwheel."

—CREED, "ULTIMATUM" (S7E13)

There's no shame in dreaming big, but sometimes you have to start small. Though Creed may not always act appropriately for his advanced age (and sometimes he rebels against it, like when he dyes his hair with black printer ink), he's at least being fairly reasonable with his wholesome resolution in "Ultimatum" (S7E13). He's not looking to become a gymnast at this point in his life, he just wants to do a single, well-executed cartwheel—and he doesn't even need anyone to make a fuss! Pin this quote to the top of *www.creedthoughts.gov.www/creedthoughts*.

In "Morrocan Christmas" (S5E11), though it's played for laughs, Meredith's New Year's resolution is a solid step toward gradually making a change for the better: "I'm not going to drink anymore. During the week." Though she follows this up with drunkenly setting her hair on fire, she still deserves credit for her realistic approach. You shouldn't expect to cross the finish line in a single bound. But every step (or cartwheel) forward means you're moving in the right direction.

Oscar Nuñez as
Oscar in Season 3.

"I love a good quitting story. It makes me feel like I have control over my own life. Gives me hope. Maybe I will have one of my own someday."

—Oscar,
"Two Weeks" (S5E21)

Oscar's eagerness to hear every juicy detail of Michael's quitting story in "Two Weeks" (S5E21) reveals that he, like so many other 9-to-5ers, is a dreamer. Living vicariously through others is something we all do from time to time, whether it's fantasizing about quitting a job or just telling someone you're not gonna put up with their BS anymore. You may have to wait a while for your own moment to come, but you can use the boldness of those brave souls as inspiration in the meantime.

Good Intentions Can Have Terrible Results...

As they say, sometimes the best-laid plans of mice and men become a sprawling mess of chili on the carpet.

D espite being a massive hit resulting in numerous incarnations around the world, the appeal of *The Office* is not universal. A common reason given by those who have tried but failed to enjoy the show is that the awkwardness and secondhand embarrassment are just too much to endure. But for fans who can stomach it, one of the funniest misfortunes in the whole series is also a reminder that even if you try to do something nice, it can backfire spectacularly.

"The trick is to undercook the onions," Kevin reveals as he details the making of his famous chili in the iconic cold open of "Casual Friday" (S5E26). Moments later, disaster strikes, and all those ingredients in the pot (and the chef himself) wind up all over the office floor. The juxtaposition of Kevin's narration over the whole ordeal—staying up late the night before, pressing garlic, toasting his own ancho chiles—makes the moment even more tragic. It's a pure, kind gesture Kevin extends "at least once a year" that the employees of Dunder Mifflin Scranton surely appreciate. And then, as can happen with the best intentions, all that effort ends up seeping into the carpet.

Things simply fall apart for no good reason sometimes. When that happens, you just have to grab the nearest manila folder and do your best to pick up the pieces and move on. No use crying over spilled chili, even if making it is probably the thing you do best.

John Krasinski as Jim, Jenna Fischer as Pam, Brian Baumgartner as Kevin, Ed Helms as Andy and Steve Carell as Michael in "Fun Run Part 2"(S4E2).

...And Unfortunate Events Can Have Positive Outcomes

The Office features many moments that prove it's always worth looking for the silver lining.

When "Fun Run Part 1" (S4E1) kicks off with Michael accidentally hitting Meredith with his car, it doesn't seem like the type of thing that will work out for the best. Not only does the Scranton branch manager drive straight into one of his employees on company property, he tries to downplay it and point the blame elsewhere (more on pg. 46). But had Michael's carelessness not sent Meredith to the hospital, her rabies diagnosis may not have come in time, if at all. It's a wild ride, but it's an example of how even the stormiest clouds can have a silver lining.

This dynamic is in action throughout "Company Picnic" (S5E28), which sees the titular Dunder Mifflin event turn from fun to dark in a hurry. Though Holly and Michael's *Slumdog Millionaire*-inspired skit results in them accidentally revealing corporate's plan to shut down the Buffalo branch, the bad news is overshadowed by the fact that the two former lovebirds are finally back on the same page and in the same place after Holly's difficult transfer to Nashua. And though the Scranton branch's success as a volleyball team comes to a halt when their MVP gets injured, Pam's trip to the hospital—much like Meredith's before—goes from terrible to terrific, as she and Jim find out they're going to be parents.

Even the most optimistic among us can struggle to see the potential for a positive in the thick of a bad situation. And not everyone's luck turns around as easily as it does on a TV show. All you can do is hope that things work out that way—sometimes, they will.

Angela Kinsey as Angela, Robert R. Shafer as Bob Vance, Phyllis Smith as Phyllis and Steve Carell as Michael in "Fun Run Part 2"(S4E2).

Phyllis Smith as Phyllis and Robert R. Shafer as Bob Vance in "Roy's Wedding" (S9E2).

"I just think we all deserve to be with someone who wants to be with us."

—Phyllis,
"Crime Aid" (S5E5)

In "Crime Aid" (S5E5), Phyllis imparts this sage advice to Dwight, who's desperate to get back together with Angela despite her engagement to Andy. Phyllis's words ring undeniably true coming from the woman married to Bob Vance, Vance Refrigeration (Robert R. Shafer), a man who's never shy about showing his affection (yes, the couple gets a bit carried away with their PDA sometimes). It can be very hard to let go, but you should never have to work overtime to convince someone you're worthy of love.

Steve Carell as Michael in "Moroccan Christmas" (S5E10).

Don't Make a Promise You Can't Keep

Take it from Michael: There are few feelings worse than failing to do what you say you will.

The mere mention of "Scott's Tots" (S6E12) is enough to make many fans of *The Office* recoil. Start singing "Hey Mr. Scott, whatcha gonna do?/ Whatcha gonna do, make our dreams come true!" and they'll likely run away in terror with their hands over their ears. Both admirably kind-hearted and disastrously ill-conceived, Michael's unrealized grand gesture to pay an entire class's college tuition is an excruciating reminder of just how important it is to keep your word.

"I've made some empty promises in my life," Michael reflects as he realizes it's time to face the music, "but hands-down, that was the most generous." As he sits in the classroom enduring student performances in his honor and speeches celebrating him as a "dream-maker," the Dunder Mifflin Scranton regional manager shoots increasingly uncomfortable glances at the camera. When one student says the gift of paid tuition will give him the opportunity to "become the next President Obama," Michael breaks down in tears. Finally, as he stands before the class and looks into the hopeful eyes of the high school seniors he's about to let down, he comes clean, admitting that he was stupid for making such a promise. After a moment of stunned silence, the students understandably erupt into cacophony.

As fans of *The Office* know too well, people who mean well can still end up creating major messes (see pg. 118). Michael, as foolish as he was for promising to pay for a group of kids to go to college, clearly just wanted to make a positive impact. But good intentions can easily look cruel in hindsight if a promise is broken. Don't overpromise if you know you're going to underdeliver.

Steve Carell as Michael in "Dunder Mifflin Infinity" (S5E10).

John Krasinski as Jim and Jenna Fischer as Pam in "Dinner Party" (S4E13).

Break Out of Your Bubble

A change of scenery can sometimes yield life-changing results.

Despite being named after a small, sterile place that all but ensures mundanity, *The Office* tends to reward both its characters and viewers any time they're willing to go beyond the walls of Dunder Mifflin Scranton. Some of the most memorable episodes take place outside the confines of the titular office, from Pam's fearless fire walking at the lake in "Beach Games" (S3E23) to the claustrophobic awkwardness inside the homelife of Jan and Michael in "Dinner Party" (S4E13). The series makes clear that there are benefits to breaking out of your comfort zone, just as there are risks to staying put.

From the time her artistic side is introduced in the series, it's clear that Pam can't truly chase her vibrant ambitions from behind the reception desk. Aside from Michael, the characters who attend her art show in "Business School" (S3E17) either don't know how to appreciate her paintings (Roy) or simply refuse to (Oscar and Gil). So come Season 5, when Pam decides to pursue her passion in earnest and leave Scranton for a three-month art program at Pratt Institute in NYC, it seems she's making a wise decision. Initially, she flourishes, eagerly telling Jim about what she's learning and the friends she's making. But having to relay this info to her then-fiancé over the phone with limited time and a long distance between them, Pam begins to realize art school in the Big Apple is a different type of learning experience than she expected. Eventually, she's able to determine that she doesn't want a career in digital design. Moreover, her time away helps her fully appreciate the life she had already been building with Jim in Scranton. But without breaking out of her bubble and digging into this new experience, Pam may have never come to these conclusions and instead stayed under the heavy clouds of "What if?" that can loom over anyone who's never taken a chance.

By the series finale, it's clear that many of the characters are thriving due to their decision to explore life beyond working at Dunder Mifflin and living in Scranton. Michael has the family he's always dreamed of with Holly in Colorado, Jim and Darryl have great success with Athlead and Stanley finally finds happiness living the retired life in Florida. There's no shame in enjoying the comforting familiarity of your bubble—just make sure it's not stunting your growth.

Leslie David Baker as Stanley and Rainn Wilson as Dwight in "Beach Games" (S3E23).

Paul Lieberstein as Toby and Phyllis Smith as Phyllis in "A.A.R.M." (S9E22).

"Your computer screen can be a big strain on your eyes, so uh, it's also recommended that you step away for about...about 10 minutes every hour."

—Toby,
"Safety Training" (S3E20)

Though not the most charismatic vessel for wisdom, Toby does provide some solid advice for modern living in "Safety Training" (S3E20)—even if it is straight from a corporate manual. Whether we're working, watching YouTube videos or creating a flying version of ourselves in *Second Life*, most of us are guilty of spending too much time staring at screens. Do as Toby suggests: Take a little time away from tech each day to give your eyes and brain a break.

Steve Carell as Michael in "The Convention" (S3E2).

Never Underestimate Someone

"Well, maybe next time you will estimate me."

—MICHAEL, "THE CONVENTION" (S3E2)

Some sitcoms present characters as so imbecilic, viewers wonder how they could possibly maintain employment or even function in day-to-day life. *The Office* is not one of those shows. For all his flaws and amusing malaprops, Michael is periodically shown to be undeniably good at his job.

When he delivers this quip to Jan in "The Convention" (S3E2), the regional manager is emboldened by the fact that he was able to steal a major client away from Staples. In "Did I Stutter?" (S4E16), Michael's authority is tested when Stanley is blatantly insubordinate—and after spending the episode figuring out how to handle the conflict, Michael shows real managerial skill when he calmly but sternly reminds Stanley that he's the boss and cannot be spoken to that way. And in perhaps his most business-savvy moment in the entire series, Michael rejects David Wallace's offers to buy out the Michael Scott Paper Company in favor of getting himself, Pam and Ryan rehired (and in Pam's case, promoted) at Dunder Mifflin (more on pg. 144). If you take someone for a fool, they just might surprise you. And then you'll look like a fool.

Leslie David Baker as Stanley, Creed Bratton as Creed and Jenna Fischer as Pam in "Michael Scott Paper Company" (S5E23).

Craig Robinson as Darryl, John Krasinski as Jim and Paul Lieberstein as Toby in "The List" (S8E1).

Bet on Yourself

As proven by several characters on *The Office*, sometimes believing you can do something is the most important step toward actually pulling it off.

I n "New Boss" (S5E20), Michael makes one of the boldest decisions of the series. After suffering through the seriousness of the new Dunder Mifflin VP Charles Miner and the cancellation of his party celebrating 15 years at the company, Michael drives to New York to bring his concerns to David Wallace directly. David understands the Scranton regional manager's frustrations and even agrees to give him a company-funded anniversary party, but shockingly, Michael quits, telling the Dunder Mifflin CFO, "You have no idea how high I can fly."

Soon after, Michael becomes the Wright brothers of paper entrepreneurs as he prepares the Michael Scott Paper Company for takeoff. His bold confidence even inspires Pam to bet on herself, as the longtime receptionist is the only one at the Scranton office to take Michael up on the opportunity to go rogue. Though it is short-lived, the Michael Scott Paper Company turns out to be an incredible bargaining chip used to ensure job security for the former Dunder Mifflin employees who dared to become the competition. Michael, Pam and Ryan (who, unlike the others, had nothing to lose) bet on themselves—and against all odds, they won big.

Whether or not he was inspired by his boss and his wife's daring venture, Jim's Season 9 decision to go all in on his sports marketing company with his college friends is reminiscent of Michael's example. The affable salesman quite literally bets on himself when he invests a hefty sum of money into getting Athlead (later renamed Athleap) off the ground (though he definitely should've talked to Pam about that first, more on pg. 14). Like Michael does with Pam, Jim even convinces Darryl to take an ath-leap of faith and join him. Come the finale, the two are fully rewarded for their ambition as viewers learn Athleap has become a booming subsidiary of Converse. If the timing feels right, take a big chance. You might be surprised how high you can fly.

John Krasinski as Jim and Craig Robinson as Darryl in "Livin' the Dream" (S9E23).

Paul Lieberstein as Toby, Craig Robinson as Darryl, Catherine Tate as Nellie, Ellie Kemper as Erin, Oscar Nuñez as Oscar, Brian Baumgartner as Kevin, Jenna Fischer as Pam and John Krasinski as Jim in "Free Family Portrait Studio" (S8E24).

"Anything can happen to anyone. It's just random."

—Nellie,
"Get the Girl" (S8E19)

Despite growing up poor in England and having little in the way of formal education and job experience, as she details in "Get the Girl" (S8E19), Nellie (Catherine Tate) finds herself in a small American city working a respectable job. And according to her, that's just the luck of the draw. She's right—not every event can be traced back to rhyme or reason. Life just happens sometimes, so be ready to roll with it.

Steve Carell as
Michael and
Rainn Wilson as
Dwight in "The
Return" (S3E14).

Keep Fighting for What You Want...

The Office proves that the key to achieving a dream is often simply refusing to give it up.

Perseverance is essential when working at a small paper company. Whether you're a salesman trying to win over a big client or a warehouse manager trying to keep deliveries at a competitive pace, it takes plenty of stamina and a perseverance to succeed. Perhaps that's why so many of Dunder Mifflin's big dreamers are able to stay in the fight until they get what they want.

Throughout the series, Dwight never gives up on his quest for a more prominent position at the company. He constantly corrects any mention of his title, desperate to drop the "to the" from "assistant to the regional manager." In "The Coup" (S3E3), the bespectacled salesman even secretly meets with Jan in an attempt to overthrow Michael (we know you didn't have an appointment with your dentist named "Crentist," Dwight). Eventually, that persistence pays off as the series ends with Dwight sitting at the desk he's always dreamed of, serving as the regional manager of Dunder Mifflin Scranton.

The traits required for the trade also seem to carry over to the personal lives of Dunder Mifflin employees. Even after they get together, Jim and Pam don't stop fighting for their relationship, from enduring difficult periods of long distance to agreeing to cathartically fight it out on Valentine's Day after months of mounting issues. And while he goes about much of it so poorly, Michael never gives up on his pursuit to get back together with Holly after she moves to Nashua and starts dating A.J. (Rob Huebel). He's even willing to fight any of his employees who manage to win her over with their own proposals leading up to the moment he asks her to marry him. With a similar combo of persistence and resilience, you might realize your own dreams.

Steve Carell as Michael
and Amy Ryan as Holly in
"Garage Sale" (S7E19).

Steve Carell as Michael
and Jenna Fischer as
Pam in "Classy Christmas
Part 1" (S7E11).

...But Recognize When It's Quitting Time

As some characters learn the hard way, not everything is worth fighting for.

A s admirable as they are for refusing to give up when chasing a goal, the characters of *The Office* don't always exhibit the important flip side of that quality: knowing when it's time to throw in the towel. For years, Jim's pranks on Dwight are successful, giving him the confidence to take them to increasingly outlandish levels. But when a snowball to the face causes an angry Dwight to challenge him to a proper snowball fight in "Classy Christmas Part 1" (S7E11), Jim should have taken his cheap win and requested a truce. Instead, he accepts, only to end up locked out of the office building as Dwight emerges from a snowman and unloads a flurry of snowballs. At the end of the episode, Jim's comeuppance takes the form of paranoia when he runs through an army of decoy snowmen in the parking lot as Dwight watches from the roof.

While Jim's refusal to quit while he's ahead results in a bloody nose and embarrassment, it pales in comparison to the damage done by Michael's inability to call it quits with Jan. To the women of the office, it's easy to see that Michael and Jan's relationship is toxic, and the likes of Pam, Phyllis and Karen all encourage their boss to bail in Season 3. Unfortunately, Michael is easily won over by a change in Jan's attitude (and neckline), and by Season 4, the two are living together. In what many fans consider the most cringe-inducing episode of the series, "Dinner Party" (S4E13), the tumultuous relationship finally boils over. Though he tries to brush it all off, Michael's employees can finally see just how awful his home life with Jan is. She makes him sleep on a small cot despite having a huge bed. She plays a CD of original music by her former assistant Hunter and sings along to a song that's clearly about an affair the two had. Finally, she caps off an argument by throwing his Dundie, shattering the illusion of their happy home as well as his prized 14-inch plasma TV. This all could've been avoided had Michael just listened to everyone (and his own gut) and ended the relationship much sooner.

Endurance is commendable when you're trying to make something happen. Ending things, however, can be even more impressive. Don't push a pursuit past your breaking point.

Melora Hardin as Jan and
Steve Carell as Michael in
"Valentine's Day" (S2E16).

Steve Carell as Michael in "Finale Part 1 and Part 2" (S9E26).

"Make friends first, make sales second, make love third. In no particular order."

—Michael, "New Leads" (S6E20)

Like many things Michael says throughout the series, this line from "New Leads" (S6E20) contains a nugget of wisdom buried beneath a layer of nonsense. The ranking of important matters is not universal. It's your life; you can choose how to prioritize the professional and personal aspects, and you can always shuffle those priorities as you see fit. It's all circumstantial.

Jenna Fischer as Pam and John Krasinski as Jim in "Niagara Part 2" (S6E5).

Always Have a Backup Plan

"The boat was actually plan C, the church was plan B and plan A was marrying her a long, long time ago."

—JIM, "NIAGARA PART 2" (S6E5)

Everyone wants their wedding to be the most perfect day possible. But while Jim and Pam have grand plans for their big day, they also know their guests are more than capable of causing chaos. Fortunately, they have backup plans in place.

As soon as they arrive in Niagara Falls, things start to go off the rails: Jim accidentally reveals his bride-to-be's pregnancy, causing her grandmother's outrage, Andy suffers a dance-induced groin injury and Pam's mother Helene (Linda Purl) bemoans Pam's father's much younger date. It all seems to come to a head when Pam's veil rips—but Jim, proving the importance of improv (see pg. 6), picks up a pair of scissors and cuts his tie in half. Moments later, we're reminded that the bride and groom aren't just quick thinkers, they're wise planners: Regretting their decision to invite friends and family, Jim and Pam ditch the church ceremony in favor of privately tying the knot aboard the *Maid of the Mist*. When you have a destination you really need to reach, it's best to plan several ways to get there.

The cast during shooting of "Niagara Part 1 and Part 2" (S6E4 and S6E5).

Jenna Fischer as Pam and John Krasinski as Jim in "Money Part 1" (S4E7).

"Be strong, trust yourself, love yourself and conquer your fears. Just go after what you want and act fast because life just isn't that long."

—Pam, "Finale Part 1 and Part 2" (S9E26)

When Pam offers this powerful advice at the conclusion of "Finale Part 1 and Part 2" (S9E26), viewers can clearly see the happiness and fulfillment that can be achieved through doing exactly what she suggests. As the former receptionist knows, it can take a while to muster the courage necessary to chase your biggest dreams. But once you have enough fuel in the form of self-assurance, you can't waste another minute.

Ed Helms as Andy, Rainn Wilson as Dwight and John Krasinski as Jim in "Christmas Wishes" (S8E10).

Your Worst Enemy Can Become Your Best Friend

With enough time, even your most strongly held opinions and bitter feelings can change for the better.

A first-time viewer of *The Office* probably wouldn't predict that Jim and Dwight would wind up such good pals by the finale, which is fair given that the two probably should've been arrested for some of the things they did to each other. But through all their pranks and one-upmanship over the years, there's an obvious camaraderie blossoming between the supposed foes—look no further than "After Hours" (S8E16), in which the two eat bananas Foster together on a hotel bed after a weird night involving Cathy's (Lindsey Broad) shameless advances and imaginary smug bed bugs. In "Finale Part 1 and Part 2" (S9E26), speaking as the new regional manager, Dwight is candid when addressing the beautiful evolution of his workplace relationships: "My top salesman, Jim Halpert, was best man at my wedding, and office administrator Pamela Beesly-Halpert is my best friend. So...yes. I'd say I have gotten along with my subordinates." To top it off, he shows his love for Jim and Pam with one final act of kindness: Rather than allowing the couple to quit, he fires them so they can receive a hefty severance package.

Even the general perception of the Dunder Mifflin Scranton office itself changes for the better by the end of the series. Selling paper was clearly never Jim's passion, but without it, he wouldn't have the things he is passionate about. "Even if I didn't love every minute of it," he reflects in "Finale Part 1 and Part 2" (S9E26), "everything I have, I owe to this job. This stupid, wonderful, boring, amazing job." And despite moving on to greener pastures, Darryl recognizes just how bittersweet the goodbye really is: "Every day when I came into work, all I wanted to do was leave. So why in the world does it feel so hard to leave right now?"

Whether it's a person you can't stand or a job you hate, there's a reason it's recommended to keep enemies closer than friends. Sometimes, your real friends are the enemies you made along the way.

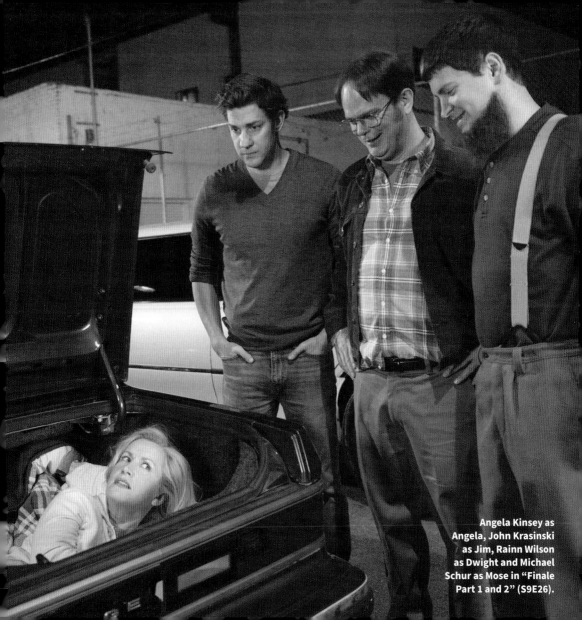

Angela Kinsey as Angela, John Krasinski as Jim, Rainn Wilson as Dwight and Michael Schur as Mose in "Finale Part 1 and 2" (S9E26).

Ed Helms as Andy in "Finale Part 1 and Part 2" (S9E26).

> "I wish there was a way to know you're in the good old days before you've actually left them."
>
> —Andy,
> "Finale Part 1 and
> Part 2" (S9E26)

Perhaps the most profound words ever uttered by the Nard Dog, this line speaks volumes to anyone who's ever felt the sting of nostalgia. But good news, Andy—there is a way to know. You just have to stop and admire the things that bring you joy. Appreciate the people you're with while you're still with them. If you've got it good, say so. That way, when you look back years down the road, you'll know you lived those days to the fullest.

**The cast of *The Office*
in a promotional
photo for Season 5.**

Photo Credits

TREVOR COURNEEN is a writer, editor and the author of *Everything I Need to Know I Learned from Bruce Springsteen.* His credits include various pop culture features for *Paste* as well as special projects for *Time Life* and *Newsweek.* When he isn't creating content for Media Lab Books, he enjoys playing with his band Deep Wimp and trying to channel Scrantonicity's energy as much as possible. He and his wife live in Brooklyn.

Media Lab Books
For inquiries, contact customerservice@topixmedia.com

Copyright 2024 Topix Media Lab

Published by Topix Media Lab
14 Wall Street, Suite 3C
New York, NY 10005

Printed in China

ISBN-13: 978-1-956403-76-3
ISBN-10: 1-956403-76-0

CEO Tony Romando

Vice President & Publisher Phil Sexton
Senior Vice President of Sales & New Markets Tom Mifsud
Vice President of Retail Sales & Logistics Linda Greenblatt
Vice President of Manufacturing & Distribution Nancy Puskuldjian
Digital Marketing & Strategy Manager Elyse Gregov

Chief Content Officer Jeff Ashworth
Senior Acquisitions Editor Noreen Henson
Creative Director Susan Dazzo
Photo Director Dave Weiss
Executive Editor Tim Baker
Managing Editor Tara Sherman

Content Editor Trevor Courneen
Content Designer Glen Karpowich
Associate Editor Juliana Sharaf
Designers Alyssa Bredin Quirós, Mikio Sakai
Copy Editor & Fact Checker Madeline Raynor
Assistant Photo Editor Jenna Addesso
Assistant Managing Editor Claudia Acevedo

1C-C24-1